Nature's Monuments

Samantha Bell

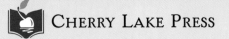
CHERRY LAKE PRESS

Published in the United States of America by Cherry Lake Publishing Group
Ann Arbor, Michigan
www.cherrylakepublishing.com

Reading Adviser: Beth Walker Gambro, MS, Ed., Reading Consultant, Yorkville, IL

Photo Credits: cover, title page: © Gary C. Tognoni/Shutterstock; page 4: NPS Photo; page 5: NPS Photo; page 7: © Hjg1970/Dreamstime.com; page 8: NPS Photo; page 11: NPS Photo; page 12: NPS Photo/Jacob W. Frank; page 13: © Kwiktor/Dreamstime.com; page 14: © Danita Delimont/Shutterstock; page 15: NPS Photo; page 17: © Photoxite/Dreamstime.com; page 18: NPS Photo/Lucas Barth; page 19: © Kelly Vandellen/Dreamstime.com; page 21: © Alysta/Dreamstime.com; page 22: NPS Photo; page 23: NPS Photo; page 24: © Anton Foltin/Dreamstime.com; page 25: NPS Photo; page 27: Mike Doukas, Public domain, via Wikimedia Commons; page 29: © Dene' Miles/Shutterstock; page 30: © motortion/Dreamstime.com

Cherry Lake Press is an imprint of Cherry Lake Publishing Group.

Library of Congress Cataloging-in-Publication Data

Names: Bell, Samantha, author.
Title: Nature's monuments / written by Samantha Bell.
Description: Ann Arbor, Michigan : Cherry Lake Publishing, 2024. | Series: National park adventures | Audience: Grades 4-6 | Summary: "Explore the majestic places that many flock to see with their own eyes. From Dinosaur National Monument to Craters of the Moon, readers will discover what forces helped shape incredible natural features. Part of our 21st Century Skills Library, this series introduces concepts of natural sciences and social studies centered around a sense of adventure"— Provided by publisher.
Identifiers: LCCN 2023010576 | ISBN 9781668927434 (hardcover) | ISBN 9781668928486 (paperback) | ISBN 9781668929957 (ebook) | ISBN 9781668931431 (pdf)
Subjects: LCSH: National parks and reserves—United States—Juvenile literature. | Natural monuments—United States—Juvenile literature.
Classification: LCC E160 .B454 2024 | DDC 917.3—dc23/eng/20230327
LC record available at https://lccn.loc.gov/2023010576

Cherry Lake Publishing Group would like to acknowledge the work of the Partnership for 21st Century Learning, a Network of Battelle for Kids. Please visit http://www.battelleforkids.org/networks/p21 for more information.

Printed in the United States of America
Corporate Graphics

Note from publisher: Websites change regularly, and their future contents are outside of our control. Supervise children when conducting any recommended online searches for extended learning opportunities.

Samantha Bell was born and raised near Orlando, Florida. She grew up in a family of eight kids and all kinds of pets, including goats, chickens, cats, dogs, rabbits, horses, parakeets, hamsters, guinea pigs, a monkey, a raccoon, and a coatimundi. She now lives with her family in the foothills of the Blue Ridge Mountains, where she enjoys hiking, painting, and snuggling with their cats Pocket, Pebble, and Mr. Tree-Tree Triggers.

CONTENTS

Introduction

The National Park Service protects national monuments. National monuments are different from national parks. One of the main differences is the reason for protecting the land. National parks are protected because they are scenic, educational, and recreational places. National monuments have historical, cultural, or scientific value. Still, some national monuments are just as unique and beautiful as the national parks. Fossils, volcanoes, and rock bridges are only a few of the many natural monuments.

CHAPTER 1

Dinosaur National Monument

Utah and Colorado

In 1909, **paleontologist** Earl Douglass was on a mission. He was searching for dinosaur bones. They would go on display in the Carnegie Museum of Natural History in Pittsburgh, Pennsylvania. Douglass searched the Morrison Formation. This huge rock formation extends throughout the western United States. After many weeks, Douglass discovered eight bones from the tail of an apatosaurus. As he dug up the bones, he found more fossils. The Carnegie Quarry was established. During the next 13 years, the museum funded **excavations** at the quarry. Douglass oversaw all the work. More than 350 tons (317.5 tonnes) of fossils were found in his small section.

View from an overlook in Dinosaur National Monument

150-million-year-old fossils at the Quarry Exhibit Hall in Dinosaur National Monument

Douglass's dinosaur bones were one of the most important dinosaur discoveries of the 20th century. In 1915, Dinosaur National Monument was created to protect 80 acres (32 hectares) of the quarry. Visitors to the monument can see actual dinosaur bones. The Quarry Exhibit Hall has a wall of approximately 1,500 bones. The bones have been partially uncovered. They can be easily seen in the rock. They include bones from allosaurus, apatosaurus, and stegosaurus. In some places, visitors can touch the fossils.

In 1938, the Dinosaur National Monument was expanded to include another 200,000 acres (80,937 ha). Most of this land is wilderness. It includes the Green and Yampa rivers. That way, those **ecosystems** would also be protected.

Dinosaur National Monument also preserves cultural histories of early **Indigenous** peoples. Archaeologists have found petroglyphs and pictographs from prehistoric tribes. Petroglyphs are rock carvings made with a stone chisel and hammerstone. Pictographs are cave paintings. Some show human figures. Others are of animal figures, such as birds, snakes, lizards, and bighorn sheep. Still other designs include circles and spirals. Several areas in the monument allow visitors to view these designs.

GETTING IT TOGETHER

Paleontologists are still finding new fossils at Dinosaur National Monument. In 2010, a team of paleontologists made an exciting discovery at Cedar Mountain Formation in the park. They found the skulls of a new type of **sauropods**. The scientists named the dinosaur *Abydosaurus mcintoshi*. The discovery was especially unusual. Because of their long necks, sauropods had skulls with thin bones held together by soft tissue. When the dinosaurs died, their skulls often broke easily and fell apart quickly. But this time, scientists found four skulls. Two of them were complete.

The fossils were found in a spot overlooking the Green River. *Abydos* is the Greek name for an Egyptian city along the Nile River. The god Osiris's head and neck are said to be buried there. The rest of the name, *mcintoshi*, was named in honor of Dr. John S. McIntosh, an important researcher and contributor to Dinosaur National Monument and the study of sauropods.

CHAPTER 2

Craters of the Moon National Monument and Preserve

Idaho

Craters of the Moon is a vast area of lava flows. But the lava did not come from one large volcano. Instead, it flowed from fissure **eruptions**. The eruptions occurred along cracks in Earth's crust. This series of cracks is known as the Great Rift. Gases easily escaped through the cracks. Without the pressure of the gases, the eruptions were very mild. They produced the lava flows. Small **cinder cones** formed, too. Today, the site contains more than 1,000 square miles (2,590 square kilometers) of lava flows and other volcanic features. The national monument was created to protect this unusual landscape.

A series of sinks or pit craters, where solidified lava collapsed into an empty chamber beneath it

The last eruptions occurred 2,100 years ago. But the volcanoes are not dead, just **dormant**. Geologists believe that the area will become active again within the next 1,000 years. But for now, visitors to Craters of the Moon can explore many volcanic features. The site has more than 25 cinder cones. Each one is a small volcano. Visitors can also find tree molds. These are impressions that formed when lava flowed around a tree. The site also has many caves. Most of the caves are lava tubes. These are natural tunnels that the lava flowed through underground. Four of these caves are open for visitors to explore.

Inside Indian Tunnel is one of the tube caves visitors can explore in Craters of the Moon National Monument.

The volcanic landscape of Craters of the Moon
National Monument

The monument's name came from an explorer named Robert Limbert. He visited the area and then wrote a magazine article about it. He called it Craters of the Moon, and it became official in 1924. Craters of the Moon does have some connections with space. In 1969, Apollo 14 astronauts spent some time training at Craters of the Moon. The moon also has a volcanic landscape. The astronauts had to learn which volcanic samples were the most valuable. They also had to understand what they were exploring. That way, they could describe it to the geologists back on Earth.

BLOOMING ON THE MOON

From late spring until September, wildflowers grow in the lava fields. Some of the flowers that grow are only found at the park. The flowers are evenly spaced in neat rows. But no one planted them. The flowering plants have to compete for a limited amount of water. Because of this, they cannot grow close together. Their roots go down nearly 3 feet (1 meter) beneath the surface. They must reach out to gather up enough water.

Devils Tower National Monument

Wyoming

Devils Tower is a rock formation in the northwest corner of the Black Hills. It stands 1,267 feet (386 m) above the Belle Fourche River. Geologists have studied Devils Tower since the late 1800s. It is the world's largest example of columnar jointing. This type of structure is formed by lava. As lava cools, it **contracts**. This causes the rock to form cracks, or joints. The cracks continue down the rock, creating long columns. Each column may have four to seven sides. Many scientists believe that Devils Tower formed this way underground. **Erosion** eventually

Many scientists believe that Devils Tower was formed underground.

A climbing ranger ascends Devils Tower on one of its many routes.

People come from all over the world to climb Devils Tower. The first people to climb it were two local ranchers in 1893. They made a 350-foot (107 m) wooden ladder and attached it to the side of the tower. Parts of the ladder can still be seen on the side of the rock formation. Today, about 5,000 to 6,000 visitors climb Devils Tower each year. They can choose from more than 200 rock climbing routes. Climbers should watch out for snakes, poison ivy,

Devils Tower became the first national monument in 1906. But it was already an important part of Native American culture. Six tribes live in or near the region. More than 24 other tribes also have connections to the tower. Ceremonies still take place at the monument. The most common rituals are prayer offerings. These are represented by colorful cloths or bundles placed near the tower or along the park's trails. The cloths may represent an offering, a request, or a remembrance of a person or place. Visitors to the monument should not touch or disturb the prayer cloths.

A BAD TRANSLATION

The monument was not always called Devils Tower. Native Americans had their own names for the formation. The Lakota name was *Mato Tipila*, which meant "Bear Lodge." Most maps from 1857 to 1901 mark the tower as Bear Lodge. Other Native American names were translated as "Tree Rock" and "The Place Where Bears Live." The name change occurred because of an expedition by Colonel Richard Irving Dodge. A mapmaker in his group said that the Native Americans called it "bad god's tower." The name "Devils Tower" was created. Many people would like it changed back to Bear Lodge.

CHAPTER 4

Rainbow Bridge National Monument

Utah

A natural bridge is a **fragile** rock sculpture shaped like a bridge. It is formed by nature. Rainbow Bridge is one of the world's largest natural bridges. It is 290 feet (88 m) tall and 275 feet (83.8 m) across. It is located near the Navajo Mountain in Utah. Long ago, water formed the bridge through erosion. It flowed down the side of Navajo Mountain toward the Colorado River. It traveled over layers of rock. The water cut into the rock, gradually forming a hole. As it flowed through the hole, it continued to enlarge it until it had formed a bridge.

Flowing water naturally formed Rainbow Bridge over time.

Rainbow Bridge is a sacred place for many peoples Indigenous to the region.

Rainbow Bridge is tucked away deep in a canyon. Since before recorded history, Indigenous peoples viewed the bridge as a sacred place. It is associated with the traditions of six Indigenous nations, including the Hopi, Dine, and Ute, among others. It inspired origin stories and was the place where religious ceremonies were performed. It was an important part of Native culture. Then in 1909, the bridge was "officially" discovered. Two men heard about the bridge and searched for it. One was archeologist Dr. Byron Cummings. The other was surveyor William B. Douglass. Eventually, they joined together. With the help of some Ute and Paiute guides, they found the bridge.

PRESERVING THE PAST

Today, Indigenous peoples still view Rainbow Bridge as sacred. They ask that visitors not walk under or near the bridge out of respect. When Lake Powell was created, it covered up many other sacred sites around Rainbow Bridge. Some members of the Navajo Nation, or Dine, think the dam and lake are important. But others want all the water drained. They also believe the number of tourists that come each day should be limited. They want to preserve Rainbow Bridge as a sacred place.

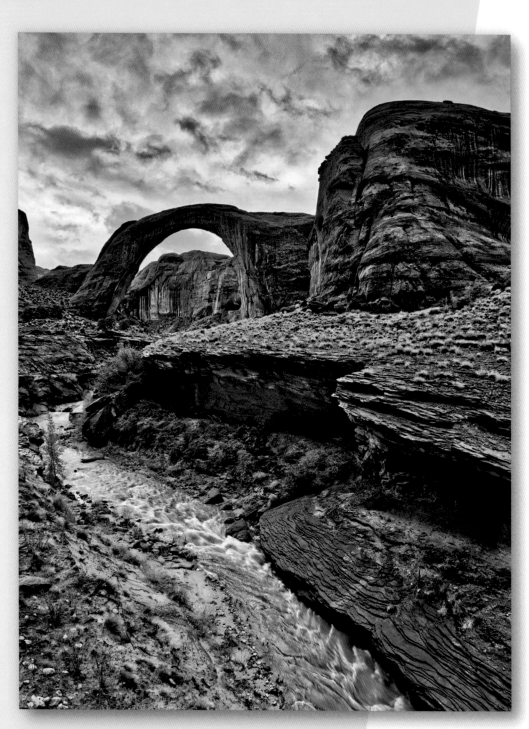

The amount of water flowing beneath Rainbow Bridge changes throughout the year.

A tour boat approaches Rainbow Bridge.

At the time, Rainbow Bridge was in one of the most remote regions in the country. People had to walk for miles up a canyon to reach it. Then in 1963, the Glen Canyon Dam was built. Water flooded the canyon, creating Lake Powell. The water is used for creating power. It also ensures that California, Arizona, and Nevada have a steady water supply. Today, the shores of Lake Powell reach the base of the bridge. Visitors can travel by boat to see the bridge. They can also hike 13 to 14 miles (20.9 to 22.5 km) to it. But the roads go through the Navajo Indian Reservation. Hikers must have a permit from the Navajo Nation to take that route.

Mount St. Helens National Volcanic Monument

Washington

Mount St. Helens is an active volcano within the Gifford Pinchot National Forest. For more than 100 years, there were no major eruptions. But on May 18, 1980, an earthquake shook the volcano. Part of the mountain collapsed in a massive avalanche. It was the largest landslide ever recorded. The avalanche released pressurized gases in the volcano. It erupted with so much force that flattened more than nearly 150 square miles (388 sq. km) of forest. At the same time, ash rose approximately 80,000 feet (24,384 m) into the sky. The mountain's glaciers and snowfields melted. Water mixed with ash to form volcanic mudflows. These poured into

The first eruption in more than 100 years of Mount St. Helens on May 18, 1980

The eruption lasted 9 hours. Wind carried ash for miles. It darkened the sky and covered the ground. The beautiful forest landscape had become empty and gray. Two years later, the mountain and surrounding areas were designated as a national monument. It included 110,000 acres (44,515 ha). As a national monument, the land would be left alone. Scientists wanted to see how nature would respond to the destruction. They wanted to know if the environment could recover on its own. The volcano continued to erupt until 1986.

THE SURVIVORS

After the Mount St. Helens eruption, everything appeared to be destroyed. But scientists found that thousands of plants, fungi, and animals had survived. Ants and other insects that were underground quickly recovered. Some **nocturnal** animals had been safely underground, too. These included bats, mice, and gophers. Rocks and cliffs protected some plants and animals from the blast. Small trees that had been buried by snow also were protected. Fish and amphibians in the water were safe. Fireweed was one of the first plants to return. It grew from the roots left under the soil.

Wildflowers growing near Mount St. Helens in the summer

Mount St. Helens has become world-famous as a natural laboratory. The landscape was destroyed in the eruption. But over the years, it has become a rich and diverse habitat again. Scientists are recording the plants and animals that have returned. They are discovering new wildlife habitats. The area around the volcano is also a place people can enjoy again. Visitors can take in the scenic views. They can explore one of the country's longest lava tubes. They can even climb to the rim of the volcano's crater. Other activities include fishing

Activity

Plan Your Adventure!

You've read about monuments with fossils, lava, and rocks. Write down the ones you found the most interesting. Then check out the other books in this series. What other places would you add to your list?

Letters from the Field

This book tells about many discoveries. Earl Douglass discovered dinosaur bones. Byron Cummings and William B. Douglass found the Rainbow Bridge. Scientists saw plants and animals returning to Mount St. Helens. Imagine you were there during one of these discoveries. Think about your five senses. What would you have seen, heard, tasted, smelled, or touched? How would you have felt? Then write a letter to a friend or family member describing what it was like.